THE POWER OF BODY LANGUAGE

Create positive impressions and communicate persuasively

Written by Rosanna Gangemi
Translated by Rebecca Neal

BODY LANGUAGE IS A POWERFUL ALLY

- **Issue:** how can I use my verbal and body language to communicate clearly and persuasively?
- **Uses:** since body language is an integral part of day-to-day communication, mastering it allows you to only express what you want to express in order to be as professional as possible at work. Understanding how it works also makes it easier to understand your colleagues' behaviour and be in tune with them.
- **Professional context:** job interviews, presentations, negotiating, client management, social contact within the company, etc.
- **FAQs:**
  - How can I hide my anxiety to seem sure of myself?
  - How can I eliminate mannerisms which unnecessarily distract the person I am talking to?
  - What attitudes should I avoid to make a less senior colleague feel comfortable?
  - How can I convince a client that my product is the best?
  - How can I present a project to my colleagues?
  - How can I interpret the behaviour of the person I am talking to?

  "The body is not mute, but it talks without us noticing it."

Who among us has not practised an interview speech until we have perfected it, only to stumble once we are in front of another person? If you are familiar with this situation and feel disheartened that you cannot control every aspect of the message you are delivering, take comfort, because it is entirely possible to learn to regulate the finer details of your body language in order to achieve your goals.

Since your facial expressions, gestures and posture seem to have as much persuasive power as your words, it is essential to spot the elements which convey states of mind, emotions or truths. These are sometimes buried deep within your subconscious, but they can nonetheless put you at a disadvantage on the big day. There is only the thinnest of lines between a meeting which turns into a fiasco and one where you dazzle your audience with your charisma and magnetism. In this case, the expression conveyed by your body language spurs your listeners to either confirm or reject their first impression of you. In poker, these interfering signals are known as 'tells', as they allow players to figure out their opponents' intentions. In the same way, a person's romantic interest in you can be confirmed through very specific micro expressions (concept developed by the American psychologist Paul Ekman, born in 1934).

In the world of work, where relationships are often based on a superficial knowledge of the other person, mastery (or relative mastery, since it is impossible to control every element of our behaviour) of body language is all the more important. It is therefore unsurprising that nonverbal communication is so highly regarded by public figures, politicians and also managers, who are constantly working on their expressiveness in order to capture people's attention and ultimately to persuade. They also often call on the services of 'gesture profilers'.

Learn to speak this language, so that its vocabulary is no longer a mystery to you.

BODY LANGUAGE: THE BASICS

"One cannot not communicate" (Watzlawick, Beavin and Jackson, 1972)

Our bodies are constantly sending information, and this represents a mode of communication in its own right. Body language can punctuate, reinforce, subtly change and even contradict what is expressed in words. This physical communication – whether voluntary or involuntary, visual (gestures, posture, etc.) or vocal (tone of voice, speed of delivery, etc.) – takes place through touch, speech, and hormonal pathways, and by means of gestures and movements which are interpreted correctly thanks to a shared culture.

THE 3 VS OF COMMUNICATION

Some apparently insignificant gestures can determine a career, as indicated in a study of 200 human resources directors carried out by the recruiter OfficeTeam in France in 2012. The study revealed that during a job interview, 90% of HR directors say that they pay attention to candidates' gestures and posture. These results echo those of one of the classic studies on the subject, namely the study carried out by Albert Mehrabian (Iranian-born American psychologist, born in 1939), which claims that an emotional message (meaning one concerning feelings or states of mind) follows the 3 Vs rule (also known as the 7%-38%-55% rule) and is:

- 55% nonverbal (visual communication);

- 38% paraverbal (vocal communication);
- and only 7% verbal (content).

The transmission of an emotional message

Nonetheless, these considerations must be qualified, because they have not been proven for all neutral speech (technical speech, classes, etc.).

CONGRUENCE

In order to optimise communication, these three forms of language must be coherent. If two kinds of speech which come from different channels and offer different signs are sent together, it is more than likely that the addressee will not receive the overall message correctly. For example, it is not recommended to shake somebody's hand and mumble "hello" without looking at them, or to say "your salary offer is absolutely fine for me" while avoiding eye contact with the other person, putting your hands over your mouth or faking a smile.

INTERPRETING PHYSICAL (NONVERBAL AND PARAVERBAL) SIGNS

Now that we are aware of the body's power of persuasion, we can analyse the grammar of the most revealing postures and gestures, as shown in positive and negative body language. Watch out, though: some gestures can have several different meanings depending on the situation!

Finally, beyond the fact that this approach allows you to understand new aspects of your communication, you must keep in mind that this knowledge of physical signals should also help you to interpret the gestures of the people you speak to. Based on a substantial body of research by leading experts in physical signals, in particular the Belgian psychologist Joseph Messinger (1945-2012), we can confirm that by being attentive to your body and to other people's bodies, you will be able to give the desired impression and interpret nonverbal messages.

The figure

- **The head.** Although most people tend to naturally tilt their heads, they do not realise the message they are sending by doing this. Tilting the head towards the right is linked to the rational side; tilting it towards the left appeals to the emotional side; finally, holding it high conveys a self-assurance and self-confidence that can go as far as contempt. It is therefore not recommended to adopt this last posture too often, at the risk of appearing aggressive and arrogant. When you are interacting with someone, make sure that your body never shows physical submissiveness: for example, a bowed head conveys giving up or defeat, and brings to mind the attitude of a pupil or a child in the face of authority. It can also reveal sadness.

- **The shoulders.** When you are sitting opposite a recruiter, you cannot look as if you have the weight of the world on your shoulders: bring them up, draw them back and relax them. Bend the torso slightly and try to always sit or stand up straight until it becomes second nature to you. You will then appear dignified and attentive.
- **The torso.** If a smile is a starting point and a handshake seals an agreement, the rest of your body must send the same message. If you want to make the other person like you and to appear more involved, turn your whole body towards them.

Avoid any stances which could seem too passive and put you at a disadvantage (sitting down, hunched over, arms dangling) or, conversely, any stances which suggest arrogance or a lack of self-confidence (head tilted back, avoiding eye contact).

Your torso should have enough space to allow you to breathe comfortably and to give the impression that you are comfortable and in control as you as are speaking.

Standing up, place your feet hip width apart. Sitting down, lay your arms on the armrests of your chair. Maintaining an elegant posture, pay attention to the space around you and open your body towards the outside. The more you project yourself into the place, the more you will give off a sense of power and impose your authority. This is an example of what is known as a 'power pose'. If you want to learn more about being aware of your movements, see the work of Dr Moshé Feldenkrais (1904-1984).

The face

- **The smile.** A 'smile' with a closed mouth, tight lips and clenched teeth certainly will not get you very far. How, then, can you tell the different between a sincere and a fake smile? A genuine smile stays on the face for a few seconds afterwards, whereas a smile on command vanishes immediately. Likewise, although it is normal to show you top teeth when you smile openly, smiles which show all the teeth (think Hollywood stars) are often false. Be careful, because if you are anxious you could feel like you are smiling when in reality your facial muscles are frozen. Try this little trick just before the meeting you are worried about: give yourself a quick face massage, with light singular movements from bottom to top. Finally, if the other person seems unwilling to return your smile, do not read too much into it for the moment.

- **The pupils.** Dilated pupils convey positive emotions, interest or availability, which can give away an attraction. Conversely, constricted pupils reveal negative emotions, such as fear, indifference, disgust or lying.
- **The eyes.** The direction a person's eyes move in says a lot about their thoughts.
  - If the eyes are looking towards the upper left, they are thinking about something that has already happened.
  - If the eyes are central and staring into space, the person is doubting or wondering.
  - If the eyes are looking towards the lower left, they are trying to choose and are having an inner dialogue.
  - If the eyes are looking to the left at medium height, they understand.

According to the Australian body language expert Allan Pease (born in 1952), men who are lying tend to lower their gaze, while women who are lying tend to look up.

The limbs

- **The arms.** The way you use your arms is a key indicator for anyone sitting opposite you. It makes them aware of how receptive you are to their speech.
  - By positioning your arms by your sides, you are showing that you are comfortable and that you are not afraid to seize any opportunities you might encounter.
  - Conversely, by crossing your arms you are sending out a negative message: you seem to be on the defensive and, consequently, unreceptive to the information you are being given.
  - If your palms are turned slightly upwards when you move your arms, you appear open and friendly.

- **The hands.** According to studies by Susan Goldin-Meadow (born in 1949) and her colleagues in the Department of Psychology at the University of Chicago, moving helps some people's brains to work better (a technique which is well-known among actors, who walk around while learning their lines): this 'externalisation' aids our mental processes. As such, in an interview, when you probably will not be able to pace around the room, feel free to gesticulate (without exaggerating) to boost your brain.

The symbolism of the hands

POSITIVE IMPRESSIONS		NEGATIVE IMPRESSIONS	
Palms visible and facing interlocutor	Inspires CONFIDENCE	Hands wedged between legs	LACK OF SELF-ASSURANCE
Hands on hips, if in an active listening position	CONSIDERATION and INTEREST	Hands on hips	DOMINATION
Placing hands together in a triangle	Pointing upwards, ACTION; pointing downwards, ATTENTION	Resting index finger on the tip of the nose	QUESTIONING
Placing forearms flat	SELF-CONFIDENCE	Crossing hands	NEED FOR PROTECTION
Placing hands along the length of the body	CASUALNESS and ELEGANCE	Keeping hands in pockets	LACK OF CONSIDERATION
Using hands to support speech	Reinforces the interlocutor's ATTENTION and MEMORY	Playing with an object (piece of paper, pen, etc.)	STRESS
Shaking hands with the palm turned slightly upwards and adapting the degree of pressure	OPENNESS and CONSIDERATION	Greeting using both hands	FRIENDSHIP and EMPATHY but may be viewed as intrusive
Hands clasped behind back	CONFIDENCE, SELF-CONTROL and POWER	Touching one part of the body (strand of hair, earlobe, etc.)	DOUBT, HESITATION, BOREDOM or DESIRE TO SEDUCE
Rubbing the hands together	OPTIMISTIC OUTLOOK	Resting index finger on the temple and thumb on the chin	BOREDOM or JUDGEMENT
Taking some notes	INTEREST	Doodling in a notebook	LACK OF ENGAGEMENT

- Furthermore, your hands have a clear 'external' force. Touch is one of the most primitive nonverbal signals: it allows you to leave a good impression from the first encounter, by creating a unique bond with the person you are talking to. You should therefore pay attention to your handshake, which is, more or less, the only physical contact that is commonly accepted in a professional setting.

THE HANDSHAKE

An effective handshake leaves a positive impression on the other person. To do this, you should avoid:

- **A limp handshake.** A limp handshake is unpleasant and is often the sign of a weak character. Nonetheless, you should not grip too hard or you might come across as aggressive or overly dominant.
- **Damp hands.** Many people panic before an important interview, and their damp handshake gives away their state of mind. A simple trick to overcome this little embarrassment is to run your hands under cold water, rub them with a bit of talcum powder or take a handkerchief to wipe them down just before your meeting.
- **An ambivalent body position.** Do not stay sitting down to shake somebody's hand, and avoid leaning across the desk. It is customary for the oldest or the most senior person to be the first to offer their hand.

- **The legs.** Although the idea that crossed legs, like folded arms, are a sign of defensiveness and distance is fairly widespread, there are some nuances to take into account:
  - Crossing them at knee level, even during an interview, is a classic position which conveys courtesy and, especially for men, a certain stylishness.
  - If the arms and legs are both crossed simultaneously, this signals that the person is closed off.
  - When the ankle of a bent leg is resting on the knee of the opposite leg, this reveals that the person is either relaxed, or competitive and efficient. Furthermore, this masculine position is not very elegant.
  - Legs which are crossed twice – whether in a standing or a sitting position – can convey unease and a desire to protect oneself.
  - Legs folded under a chair convey a certain shyness or uncertainty.
  - If you have to remain standing for a long time, for example during a presentation, it is recommended to put your weight on both legs, which stops you from supporting your weight with one hip or rocking from left to right.
- **The feet.** Although you might not think it, it is impossible for your feet to go unnoticed. Along with the hands, these are the body parts which transmit the most signals. You should therefore avoid shifting your weight from one foot to the other or, even worse, tapping your foot. Foot-tapping conveys boredom, nervousness or exasperation, and in many cases risks distracting the person you are talking to. When you are having a conversation standing up, pay particular attention to how your feet

are positioned.

The symbolism of the feet

POSITIVE IMPRESSIONS		NEGATIVE IMPRESSIONS	
Parallel and firmly planted on the ground	PRESENCE	Pressed against the legs of the chair	TIMIDITY
When sitting, feet flat on the floor and back straight	CONFIDENCE	Pointing towards the door	DESIRE TO FLEE
Pointing towards your interlocutor	DESIRE TO COMMUNICATE with them	Remaining facing the first interlocutor when a third person joins the conversation	LACK OF OPENNESS (towards the person who has just arrived)

TAILORED INTIMACY

PROXEMICS

The neologism 'proxemics' refers to the collection of observations and theories linked to the relationship that man, as a specific cultural product, has with the space around him.

According to Edward T. Hall (American anthropologist and father of proxemics, 1914-2009), who gave us this neologism, the physical distances between people determine four different spatial zones. Infringing on these zones can lead to discreet or obvious reactions of aggression or flight. Consequently, taking them into account is a valuable approach, because it permits the establishment of kind and respectful communication.

Hall's four distances

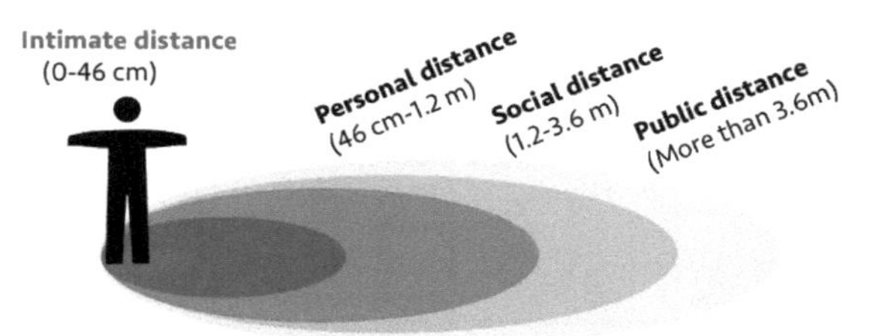

- **Intimate distance (0-46cm),** reserved for a select few (family members, partners and very close friends).
- **Personal distance (46cm-1.2m),** where we find people we get on well with (friends, colleagues who we spend time with outside the office, etc.).
- **Social distance (1.2-3.6m),** for acquaintances. At this distance, we feel safe and emotions are generally kept under control.
- **Public distance (more than 3.6m),** where interactions take place on a group level (during a meeting or a presen-

tation) or between perfect strangers.

Although this theory remains a widely-used reference point, Hall himself reminds us that the distances vary between cultures: for example, in Latin countries, and to an even greater extent in African countries, bodies are often placed closer together than in Nordic countries.

Being aware of your own personal space and of that of the person you are talking to is essential if you want to avoid making mistakes. Look at how closely they spontaneously place themselves to you at the start of your conversation and see if they move closer as it progresses. The average of these two distances will tell you the ideal amount of space to leave.

THE POLYGLOT BODY

Although anger, joy, sadness, fear, disgust and surprise can often be read on people's faces without too much difficulty, no matter what their origin or their culture, we can also observe some culture-specific features. This observation is sometimes even true among different ethnic groups within the same country. Indeed, from a phylogenetic point of view, some facial movements, which are used to express a feeling or a need, seem to be hereditary. For example, it is well known that, unlike Germanic, Scandinavian and Anglo-Saxon peoples, Mediterranean populations make greater use of the expressiveness of their bodies to communicate.

You will therefore easily understand the need to avoid intercultural clashes at crucial moments, such as during a job interview. Furthermore, before embarking on a career abroad, find out as much as possible about the habits and the customs of the country in question: this type of attention, which is perceived as a mark of respect and openness to other people, could make all the difference.

- **The particular case of Sweden.** The Swedes, who favour a plain and controlled speaking style, do not seem to be enthusiastic proponents of forms of nonverbal communication. For example, during face-to-face conversations they tend to keep a certain distance so as not to encroach on the other person's personal space. Consequently, apart from a handshake, you should avoid touching the other person.
- **The particular case of Japan.** While in Europe it seems unthinkable to not look the person you are speaking to in the eye, this is not the case in Japan. In this very hierarchical country, custom dictates that you should not look into a person's eyes, but rather at neck height. As well as this, there are some other basic rules to follow:
  - When sitting down, take care not to show the soles of your shoes (this advice also applies to Arab countries), because this is considered incredibly rude.
  - Avoid any physical contact, unless this is invited by the person you are talking to.
  - Do not force yourself to fill any silences. Although Europeans may find silences awkward, the Japanese like them and consider these moments to be very valuable.

AVOID JUMPING TO CONCLUSIONS

Morphopsychology is a method which looks for correspondences between an individual's physical appearance and their character, while morphogestural analysis explores an individual's personality by analysing their expressive and evolving physical aspects. Synergology is a new discipline in the field of communication which aims to interpret the workings of the human mind by analysing the structure of its body language. These three disciplines can all offer food for thought on the meaning of physical signals. However, they should not all be taken at face value.

Knowledge requires care and attention, so beware of hasty interpretations which can lead to misunderstandings. On the one hand, the same signal can mean several things in different sociocultural situations and contexts; on the other hand, every individual has their own way of expressing themselves. Make sure that you always put nonverbal messages into context.

To illustrate this, we can go back to the example of the symbolism of folded arms. Although many studies agree that this is a defensive gesture, the same stance can signify the opposite if the torso is particularly straight and leaning back slightly. According to the American psychologist David McNeill (born in 1933), this signals invulnerability. But it can also be a sign that the person simply wants to warm themselves up or make themselves comfortable.

TOP TIPS

- Try out the technique of mirroring. Try to put yourself in the shoes of the person you are addressing and to feel what they are feeling when they see your facial expressions, your gestures and your movements.
  - **Before an interview,** simulate real interview conditions with a person who will be critical enough for you to improve. You can also record yourself or practice in front of a mirror. This will allow you to spot the gestures that are likely to let you down on the big day.
  - **During an interview,** try to adopt a similar stance and set of gestures to your interviewer, while remaining subtle and natural. Studies – notably in the domain of neurolinguistic programming – have shown that people who are in tune with one another tend to use the same repertoire of gestures at almost exactly the same time. And it is often the case that birds of a feather flock together.
- Smile! Do not underestimate the power of a smile – one that reaches your eyes, not just your lips – during an encounter, because it indicates to other people that you are approachable, cooperative, positive and friendly.
- Be expressive. Establish and maintain direct and sincere visual contact with the other person to show them that you are attentive and open to discussion. When you offer them your hand, maintain eye contact. However, be careful not to stare too insistently at them, so as to avoid making them uncomfortable.
- Consider your handshake as your first business card.

While it is common in the business world to greet someone by shaking their hand, it is still important to accompany this gesture with a certain style, as a handshake should be firm and short.

- Favour attitudes which encourage a certain degree of openness in the person you are talking to. Position your body expansively. Research carried out at Northwestern University (2001) and Columbia University (2010) has demonstrated that, not only does our posture suffer as a result of our mood and emotional state, but it can also influence them. In other words, the act of puffing out our chest, for example, can make us feel a greater degree of pride and self-confidence. In addition, the level of testosterone – the hormone linked to wellbeing and other bywords for power – increases, while the level of the stress hormone cortisol decreases.

- Get rid of any unnecessary objects. During interviews, many people hold an object in their hands as a way of trying to channel their emotions. However, it would seem that it is wiser to keep your hands free so that they can move in harmony with what you are saying or simply rest on your thighs.

- Opt for an elegant and persuasive stance. A straight back gives the impression of presence, self-confidence and assertiveness. As such, whether you are talking one-on-one or in a group meeting around a table, hold yourself elegantly, with your spine straight, your shoulders relaxed and your head held high. When you walk, fix your eyes on a point on the horizon and look straight ahead.

- Adopt the appropriate dress code. Your choice of clothing – as well as your posture and your gestures – will be analysed by the person you are speaking to, who will not be able to disregard it. You must therefore be dressed for the job you want or, more broadly, for the context of your meeting. That said, do not overdress or you risk being seen as something you are not. During a professional encounter, the most important thing is to feel comfortable in what you are wearing and to appear tidy.

CHOOSING YOUR PERFUME

If you do not know the other person's tastes, opt for a light perfume – or even no perfume – to avoid filling the room with a fragrance that they do not like and which may subconsciously influence them.

- Make relaxation and focus your watchwords. Since it is rarely pleasant to watch face-pulling or recurring mannerisms – such as a person putting their hair behind their ear ten times, covering their mouth when they smile, or touching their neck – think about keeping in control and relaxing by breathing calmly so as not to distract the person you are talking to. Additionally, these mannerisms break your own concentration, even if you do not necessarily realise it.
- In all circumstances, favour coherent speech for maximum impact. Your verbal and nonverbal expressions should be in harmony. Your gestures, used to underline a key point and punctuate a sentence, should be perfectly synchronised with your words.

FAQS

> "Although I have realised the importance of body language and taken training to learn to control it, I still show signs of anxiety in professional situations. This visceral fear comes across in nervous gestures, a dry mouth, trembling, sweating and tense muscles. In these moments, I feel as though I'm no longer capable of controlling my own body!'

Overcoming stress is vital when important meetings appear on the horizon. To avoid sabotaging yourself, be smart in your preparation and ward off unknown situation.

- **Alleviate the visible signs of stress.** You can in fact learn to reduce this feeling of anxiety, and in doing so reduce its numerous embarrassing physical signs. Considering that potential unforeseen events fuel stress, do your best before every interview to find out about the people you will be speaking to and their aims and ambitions. At the same time, take care of your body so that you are fighting fit when you meet them. Think about resting and relaxing: relax your muscles, breathe deeply to give your body plenty of oxygen, meditate, sleep, do not overeat, etc.
- **Conquer your anxiety.** To do really thorough work, it is recommended that you undertake activities (theatre, music, dance, sports, etc.) that will force you to listen to your body 'talk' or 'express itself' and will put you in

front of an audience. The aim of this approach is to make you aware of your body's limits so that you can learn to control it. Stress will then tend to gradually dissipate during action and could even prove to be a real driving force.

In other words, turn anxiety into an asset rather than trying to kill it (which, besides, is impossible): let yourself feel it and channel it so that this tension, which you initially saw as a bad thing, changes into positive energy. Adrenaline will do the rest.

HOW CAN I ELIMINATE MANNERISMS WHICH UNNECESSARILY DISTRACT THE PERSON I AM TALKING TO?

"During our company meetings, I am in charge of presenting the status of our current projects. Even though this is a repetitive exercise, I can't manage to eliminate some mannerisms, and every time they distract me as much as they bother my audience."

Mannerisms, which in this case express a temporary feeling of anxiety, can be numerous and may vary in nature. To get rid of these inappropriate interferences, several steps are necessary:

- **Firstly, become aware of your mannerisms.** As soon as you have done this, you will have done half the job of overcoming them.
- **Secondly, take regular exercise in order to relax.** Practice relaxing disciplines, such as yoga, focusing on

your breathing, or have a relaxing massage the day before you have to speak publicly.

- **Thirdly, prepare as much as possible – but without learning the text by heart – and practice out loud to learn to enjoy persuading the audience and filling them with enthusiasm.** Excellent preparation is valuable to increase your self-confidence and enable you give a convincing performance: if you are completely in control of what you are saying, you will also control your nervous tics without noticing too much.
- **Fourthly, cultivate your charisma.** During your presentation, channel your energy into the choice of words, the intonation of your voice and the coherence of your gestures. Look the people you are talking to in the eyes, making sure that you pay everyone in your audience the same amount of attention and changing the person you are looking at from time to time (this technique is taught particularly in the entertainment industry).

You may suffer from nervous tics that are slight, involuntary and noticeable, but difficult to control, and that you constantly repeat in an identical, unpatterned and constant manner when you are speaking. You should know that your listeners will disregard these more easily than tics that you are supposed to be able to control.

WHAT ATTITUDES SHOULD I AVOID TO MAKE A LESS SENIOR COLLEAGUE FEEL COMFORTABLE?

> "I am the head of a company, and I suspect that a new employee is being bullied. I would like to talk to them about it, making sure that I inspire as much trust in them as possible, while remaining in my role as an employer."

In order to be seen as an accessible person of trust, in spite of your hierarchical superiority, learn to avoid certain gestures, attitudes and stances which may seem natural to you in other contexts:

- putting your hands behind your back or folding your arms, because this can signal that you do not want to be approached;
- avoiding eye contact, because this can convey that you do not grant much importance to what the other person is saying to you;
- shaking hands with your palm facing downwards, because this can indicate an intention to dominate;
- slouching in your chair, because this can be considered as a display of power;
- putting your hands on your hips, because this can express a degree of assertiveness that may be intimidating;
- putting your hands in your pockets, because this conveys an image of carelessness and inspires mistrust;
- encroaching on the personal space of the other person, for example by talking inches away from their face, because this can be viewed as a lack of respect and

consideration;

- not smiling, because this makes people seem serious, closed off, unlikeable and indifferent.

HOW CAN I CONVINCE A CLIENT THAT MY PRODUCT IS THE BEST?

> "I am well aware of the advantages of my product and am convinced of its effectiveness and of the fact that it would be a major asset for a potential client. However, my sales pitch and body language seem to contradict one another: my body is tense and nervous, which harms my argument and leaves me unable to convince the other person."

Wearing an elegant and understated outfit that you feel comfortable in, confidently make your way over to your client. Look them directly in the eye, smile sincerely and naturally, and offer them your best handshake (firm but gentle and with dry hands, which signal self-confidence). This is essential in order to make a positive first impression on the other person. At this stage of the encounter, it may already be possible to detect certain indicators of their personality (receptiveness, preferences, etc.).

Stabilise your stance: feet slightly apart in a V shape if you are standing up, or with your lower back pressed against the back of the chair and your chest open if you are sitting down. Position yourself opposite the client and try, without rushing them, to get as close as possible to them in order to get into their personal space.

While you are communicating the important messages, opt for measured gestures – for example, extend your hands towards your client – and try to adapt your body language to theirs (mirroring) in order to connect with them and create a personal bond. Do not lose sight of the fact that your aim is to win their trust.

Be persuasive by matching your speech to the way you look at the other person, and pay close attention in order to interpret what is not said. Observe them closely to identify the arguments and gestures that have an effect on your potential client.

HOW CAN I PRESENT A PROJECT TO MY COLLEAGUES?

> "When I present projects to my colleagues, I often get the impression that they are getting bored and that my audience is just waiting for my speech to end."

First of all, try to find out whether your audience is really getting bored by noting any unequivocal nonverbal signs: feet pointing towards the exit, looking at watches, avoiding eye contact, demonstrations of restlessness, rocking in chairs, constant changes of stance, arms folded, head down, etc. You might be judging your audience's gestures too harshly, so you should beware of hasty interpretations – for example, a finger resting on the cheek, the index finger on the temple or a slight tilting of the head are actually demonstrations of interest – which could interfere with your presentation. As a general rule, during a presentation, think about:

- **Arousing interest.** Try to constantly arouse the interest, and even the passion, of your audience. To make this possible, you must have a perfect command of the subject and believe in what you are saying, smile naturally, and remain calm and relaxed. Proceed like that and you will soon notice that your gestures match your words.
- **Creating an environment of trust.** Imagine that you are presenting your ideas to someone you trust. Hold on to the state of mind you are in after this role-playing, because it will allow you to establish a genuine relationship with your audience and charm them.
- **Inspiring a positive dynamic.** Look into your colleagues' eyes, be lively and make your presentation dynamic by taking up space. Ensure that each of your movements reflects the content of your speech and get as close as possible to your audience. The closer they feel to you, the more they will be inclined to listen and participate. Make sure that you vary your gestures, while trying to identify the emotional state of your audience.

HOW CAN I INTERPRET THE BEHAVIOUR OF THE PERSON I AM TALKING TO?

"In the company I work for, there is a very competitive atmosphere which unfortunately sometimes comes out as disloyal behaviour: holding back information, wilful misunderstandings which drive people to make mistakes, lying, etc. In this context, and to discover my colleagues' true intentions, I think that by learning to interpret their

<blockquote>behaviour accurately, I could tell the difference between true and false."</blockquote>

You must be very cautious if you want to interpret the behaviour of the person you are speaking to, because hasty and unfounded interpretations could put you in a bad position. Nonetheless, if the other person displays discomfort, nervousness or a more exaggerated degree of self-confidence than usual during your conversations, it is possible that they are not being completely honest with you.

- **Spotting discomfort.** Symbolic barriers (arms, table, etc.), a lowered head, a gaze fixed on one point, a stance which reveals the legs at a right angle to the body, fidgeting hands, narrowing eyes and more rapid blinking are all tell-tale signs of unease.
- **Spotting nervousness.** Gesticulating or repeatedly running the hands through the hair can convey a state of anxiety, especially if these gestures are accompanied by other signs, such as trembling, excessive sweating, rapid breathing, a dry mouth, etc.
- **Spotting behaviour which conceals another behaviour.** Slouching in one's chair or repeatedly yawning are behaviours which could be signs of an offhandedness designed to cover discomfort or dishonesty. Indeed, because words do not always manage to effectively persuade, those who are trying to camouflage something may resort to a set of exaggerated gestures which produce a theatrical effect and which divert people's attention, at least for a moment.
- **Spotting a lie?** Although we must always avoid drawing

conclusions based on our intuition alone, there are a number of signs which can alert us to potential dishonesty.

- ○ All displays of nervousness, especially if they are not justified, can raise questions.
- ○ Ambiguous attitudes, or any incongruity, also merit particular attention: shaking the head in contradiction with what the person is saying, the lack of a 'mirror' effect, more rapid blinking than usual, or a frown which causes little temporary wrinkles in the middle of the forehead.
- ○ Attempts to camouflage expressions are the most meaningful behaviours: rubbing the eyes for no apparent reason, covering the mouth with a hand, etc.

OVER TO YOU

Here are three exercises to drastically improve your body language.

EXERCISE 1: LIFE BEYOND YOUR FEET

When you are walking, stop staring at your feet and force yourself to keep your head held high so as to direct your gaze towards the horizon. You will develop a greater presence and a greater degree of openness to the world, while your interactions with others will completely change:

- You will naturally look straight at the person in front of you, which will give them the impression that you are interested in them and give a positive image of you. To avoid making them uncomfortable, break eye contact from time to time by looking elsewhere, to the left or the right.
- Instead of gazing timidly, you need to find a way to look at the situation head on. Why not try the following technique? Look at a point just between the eyes of the person in front of you, avoiding constantly switching from one eye to another, until you get used to the situation.

EXERCISE 2: THE NON-PARTICIPATING OBSERVER

Get settled comfortably in a place where you can watch people without necessarily having to interact with them: at a university, on public transport, in a crowd, in a bar, etc.

Carefully observe each person from their head down to their toes. What message is their body sending?

Repeat the exercise, this time while watching television.

- **Observation.** Watch a talk show, for example, with the sound muted.
- **Interpreting signals.** Next, describe each person's character traits (dominant, arrogant, authoritarian, persuasive, shy, submissive, seductive, etc.) based only on your observations about their body language. Then try to follow the same programme without the images, this time basing your interpretation only on the dialogue. Ascribe new character traits to the people whose voices you hear.
- **Results.** Do the character traits match up in both instances? Although it is more than likely that you reached the same conclusions, you probably found it easier to ascribe character traits to people by watching them than by listening to them.

EXERCISE 3: FIND THE LIMITS OF YOUR PERSONAL SPACE

To assess the boundaries of your personal space, carry out this exercise with a person you would not describe yourself as close to. Stand a few metres away from them and start a conversation. Let them gradually come closer to you until you no longer feel comfortable, then calculate the distance between you to find out the limits of your personal space.

Later, compare these results with the reality of your different day-to-day exchanges – from encounters with your
loved ones to encounters with people you do not know – to
confirm this personal space.

We want to hear from you!
Leave a comment on your online library
and share your favourite books on social media!

FURTHER READING

BIBLIOGRAPHY

- Ekman, P. (2012) *Emotions Revealed: Recognizing Faces and Feelings to Improve Communication and Emotional Life*. London: Hachette UK.
- Gevrey-Guinnebault, C. (2014), *Et si je faisais bonne impression ! Communication non verbale. Mode d'emploi*. Paris: Eyrolles.
- Goldin-Meadow, S., Levine, S. and Jacobs, S. (2014) Gesture's Role in Learning Arithmetic. In Edwards, L.D., Ferrara, F. and Moore-Russo, D. eds. *Emerging Perspectives on Gesture and Embodiment in Mathematics*. North Carolina: Information Age Publishing.
- Hall, E.T. (1988) *The Hidden Dimension*. New York: Anchor Books.
- Mehrabian, A. (1981) *Silent Messages: Implicit Communication of Emotions and Attitudes*. Belmont, California: Wadsworth.
- Messinger, J. (1994) *Ces gestes qui vous trahissent*. Paris: First Éditions.
- Messinger, J. (2002) *Le sens caché de vos gestes*. Paris: First Éditions.
- Messinger, J. (2009) *Le dico illustré des gestes*. Paris: Flammarion.
- Pease, A. (1981) *Body Language: How to Read Others' Thoughts by their Gestures*. Sydney: Camel Publishing Company.
- Tardy, M. (2012), *Morphopsychologie. Traité pratique. Lire le visage et comprendre la personnalité*. Escalquens:

Éditions Dangles.
- Watzlawick, P, Beavin, J.H. and Jackson, D.D. (2014)
  *Pragmatics of Human Communication: A Study of
  Interactional Patterns, Pathologies and Paradoxes*. New
  York: W.W. Norton and Company.

ADDITIONAL SOURCES

- Huang, L., Galinsky, A.D., Gruenfeld, D.H., Guillory, L.E.
  (2011) Powerful Posture Versus Powerful Roles: Which
  Is the Proximate Correlate of Thought and Behavior?
  Psychological Science. Volume 22, pp. 95-102.
- National Centre for Biotechnology Information
  (2010) Power posing: brief nonverbal displays affect
  neuroendocrine levels and risk tolerance. *NCBI*. 21(10),
  pp. 1363-1368.
- Website of OfficeTeam
  http://m.officeteam.fr/accueil
- Website of Joseph and Caroline Messinger
  http://www.ecoledesgestes.com/
- Website of Paul Ekman
  www.paulekman.com

50MINUTES.com